Survivor's Science in the
Desert

Peter D. Riley

HODDER
Wayland

An imprint of Hodder Children's Books

White-Thomson Publishing Ltd,
2-3 St Andrew's Place, Lewes,
East Sussex BN7 1UP

Published in Great Britain in 2003 by Hodder
Wayland, an imprint of Hodder Children's
Books

This paperback edition published in 2006

This book was produced for White-Thomson
Publishing Ltd by Ruth Nason.

For more information on this series and
other Hodder Wayland titles, go to
www.hodderwayland.co.uk

Design and illustration: Carole Binding

British Library Cataloguing in Publication Data
Peter D. Riley
    In the Desert. - (Survivor's Science)
    1. Deserts - Juvenile literature 2. Desert
    ecology - Juvenile literature 3. Desert
    survival - juvenile literature
    I. Title
    577.5'4
    ISBN 0 7502 4539 5

Printed in China by WKT Company Ltd

Hodder Children's Books
A division of Hodder Headline Limited
338 Euston Road, London NW1 3BH

Acknowledgements
The author and publishers thank the following for their permission to
reproduce photographs: Corbis: cover (David Muench) and pages 4 (Yann
Arthus-Bertrand), 9 (Dale O'Dell), 10 (David Muench), 16 (David G. Houser), 36
(Anthony Bannister; Gallo Images), 38 (Clem Haagner; Gallo Images), 41
(Michael and Patricia Fogden), 42 (Joe McDonald), 44 (Firefly Productions);
Science Photo Library: page 11 (Bernhard Edmaier); Still Pictures: pages 13
(Gordon Wiltsie), 14 (Fans Lemmens), 17 (Roger De La Harpe), 18 (Roland
Seitre), 20 (Ray Pfortner), 23 (Francois Savigny), 26 (Mathieu Laboureur), 28
(M. & C. Denis-Hout), 31 (Penny Tweedie), 32/cover (Nigel Dickinson), 33t
(Adrian Arbib), 33b (Adrian Arbib), 34 (Voltchev-UNEP), 39 (Romano Cagnon).
The science activity photographs are by Carole Binding.

Contents

Introduction

Some surprises about deserts

When people think of a desert, they may picture a hot, dry land covered in **sand dunes**. Perhaps they also imagine cacti growing and camels walking by. It is true that some deserts are very hot and dry during the day, though at night they are very cold. Deserts like this are found around the equator – the hottest region on the Earth. But there are other deserts which are cold and dry for most of the year.

Although sand is found in every desert, it does not always form dunes. Many deserts are covered in rocks as well as sand. The idea that cacti grow in every desert is also not true. Cacti only grow in parts of the North American deserts. Camels, too, are not found in every desert. Snakes and lizards are common desert animals. In Africa, elephants have been seen crossing desert land.

So, deserts can be full of surprises. Perhaps you will discover some as you turn the pages of this book.

*Desert landscapes vary. They may be covered in rocks as well as sand. This is a **wadi** in the Arabian Desert. The main feature that all deserts share is lack of rainfall.*

The keys to survival

Many towns and cities have grown up on the edges of deserts, getting most of the water and food they need from other regions. But small numbers of people have learned how to survive in the desert and have made it their home. Sometimes explorers make an **expedition** into a desert, to make maps, search for oil and study how living things can survive in the dry conditions. Before an expedition, they plan how they will survive. They study what to wear, how to travel safely, how to find the way, how to make a shelter, how to stay healthy, and, if there is an emergency, how to be rescued.

Discovering with science

For thousands of years people have investigated their surroundings and made discoveries that have helped them survive. About 400 years ago, a way of investigating called the scientific method was devised, to help us understand our world more clearly. The main features of the scientific method are:

1 Making an **observation**

2 Thinking of an idea to explain the observation

3 Doing a test or experiment to test the idea

4 Looking at the result of the test and comparing it with the idea

Today the scientific method is used to provide explanations for almost everything. In this book you can find out about the science that helps people, plants and animals survive in deserts. You can also try some activities to see how different areas of science, such as materials and light, help life survive in the driest places on Earth. In these activities you may use the whole of the scientific method or just parts of it, such as making observations or doing experiments. But you will always be using science to make discoveries.

Are you ready to find out how people survive in the desert? Turn the page to find the major deserts of the world.

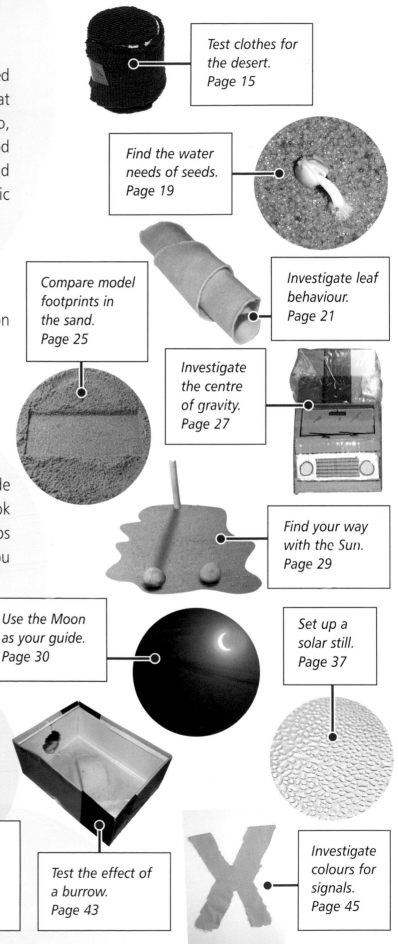

Test clothes for the desert. Page 15

Find the water needs of seeds. Page 19

Compare model footprints in the sand. Page 25

Investigate leaf behaviour. Page 21

Investigate the centre of gravity. Page 27

Find your way with the Sun. Page 29

Use the Moon as your guide. Page 30

Set up a solar still. Page 37

Test the effect of a burrow. Page 43

Investigate colours for signals. Page 45

Deserts of the world

Most deserts are near the Tropics of Cancer and Capricorn, although some are far north of the tropical region. All these areas stay very dry for most of the year.

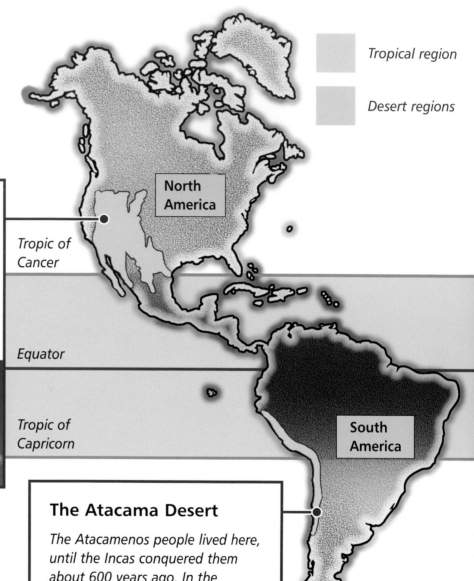

Tropical region

Desert regions

North America

Tropic of Cancer

Equator

Tropic of Capricorn

South America

The North American Deserts

These deserts were once home to Native American people such as the Hopi, Zuni, Navajo and Apache. Today a few Native Americans and people of other races also live here.

One type of plant here is the huge saguaro cactus. Other plants, such as yuccas, provide homes for animals like beetles and the Gila woodpecker.

Many types of plants and animals that live in one desert region are not found anywhere else in the world. Most deserts are also home to groups of people, who have learnt how to survive in this special environment. Some live by searching all over the desert for food and water. Some trek across parts of the desert to find food for their livestock. Some live by trading, and use camels to carry goods between distant towns.

The Atacama Desert

The Atacamenos people lived here, until the Incas conquered them about 600 years ago. In the sixteenth century expeditions from Spain arrived and more people settled in the desert. People living here today work at mining copper and other minerals.

This desert is the nesting place of many seabirds. The eggs and chicks are sometimes eaten by hog-nosed skunks and desert foxes.

The Sahara Desert

*This is the world's largest desert. About a fifth of its area is covered in sand dunes. There are **oases** where palm trees grow.*

The Sahara is home to the Tuareg, who used to transport salt across the desert on camels. Now many work in the oil industry.

Huge numbers of locusts move across the desert, eating any plants they can find.

The Gobi Desert

This is a cold desert. In summer it is as hot as other deserts, but in winter it can be −40°C and may be covered in snow. Here the Mongol people keep sheep, goats and horses and move around to find them fresh grazing.

Tamarisk trees grow here and there is a wide variety of animals, from jerboas (like hopping mice) to camels.

The Arabian Desert

The Bedouin people move around in this desert, finding fresh grazing for their flocks of sheep and herds of goats.

Africa

The Kalahari Desert

The Kalahari receives more rain than the Namib, so there is more vegetation here. There is also a wider range of animals.

Australia

The Namib Desert

The Namib and the Kalahari Deserts are home for the San (also called Bushmen). They live by gathering plant food and hunting animals.

In the Namib, a strange type of conifer called the welwitschia grows very close to the ground. It has two long leaves which spread out across the sand. Jackass penguins live on the coast. Inland live lizards, snakes and antelope.

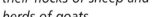

The Australian Deserts

Aborigine people have lived here for thousands of years, gathering plant food and hunting animals.

The mulga and mallee bushes are two kinds of large plants that grow here. Animals include the frilled lizard and the kangaroo.

Why are deserts dry?

At many places on the Earth water follows a path called the water cycle. At some places this cycle may stop for some time or break, and it is here that deserts form.

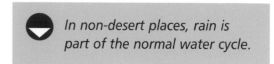

In non-desert places, rain is part of the normal water cycle.

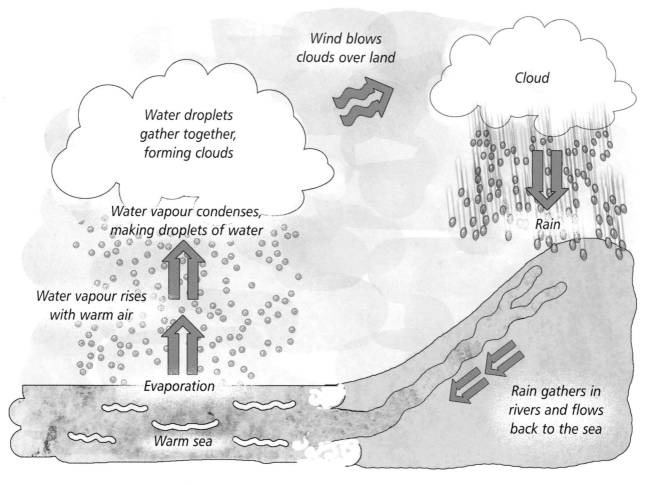

Wind blows clouds over land

Cloud

Water droplets gather together, forming clouds

Water vapour condenses, making droplets of water

Rain

Water vapour rises with warm air

Evaporation

Rain gathers in rivers and flows back to the sea

Warm sea

The water cycle

Water **evaporates** from the surface of a warm sea and becomes **water vapour** – part of the air above the sea. The warm air rises through cooler air above it, and as it rises, it cools. When the water vapour cools, it **condenses** on dust particles in the air, making droplets of water. The water droplets occur in huge numbers and form clouds.

In time, winds blow the clouds over the land. When the clouds are blown upwards, over hills, the droplets cool down some more. This makes them gather together into larger drops, which fall as rain.

The rain flows through the soil into streams and rivers, and the water is carried back to the sea.

The water cycle at the equator

When scientists look for answers to questions, they try to find patterns in the information that they have. In the map on pages 6-7, you can see a pattern in the position of most of the deserts. Some are a distance north of the equator and others are a similar distance south of the equator. The reason for this is a break in the water cycle, which happens in the following way.

The Sun's rays heat the Earth most strongly at the equator. Air over the equator becomes hot and rises, carrying water vapour with it. The water vapour cools, forms clouds and falls back to Earth as rain. The air that is left high in the sky then contains very little water vapour. It is dry air.

This dry air spreads out and moves both north and south of the equator. Eventually it sinks back to the Earth, warming up on its way. Warm, dry air therefore reaches the ground, causing any water present to evaporate – and so the ground dries out and becomes a desert.

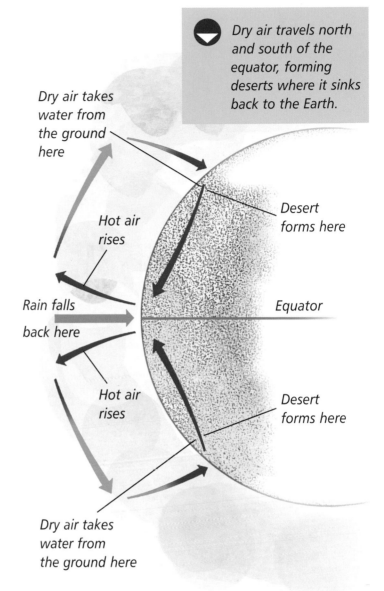

Dry air takes water from the ground here

Hot air rises

Rain falls back here

Hot air rises

Dry air takes water from the ground here

▼ Dry air travels north and south of the equator, forming deserts where it sinks back to the Earth.

Desert forms here

Equator

Desert forms here

The air does not remain over the desert but moves back to the equator. At times it may move quickly and cause **desert storms**.

◀ Desert storms may occur as warm air is blown quickly towards the equator.

Deserts far inland

The water cycle diagram on page 8 shows that, when air carrying clouds rises over a hill, rain falls and flows back to the sea. The air that is left is then dry. As it moves further overland, it has no rain to release. This explains how inland areas become deserts.

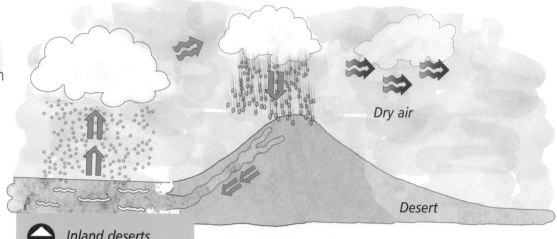

Dry air

Desert

Inland deserts form when the air has lost all its water vapour before it is blown over the land.

This kind of break in the water cycle has caused the Gobi Desert to develop. It also helps to keep the centre of the Sahara, Kalahari and Australian deserts dry.

Does it rain in the desert?

It does rain, but not often. In the Atacama Desert (one of the driest deserts), it did not rain for 401 years – between 1570 and 1971. In other deserts there may be a period of rain every year, or it may rain once every few years. Some deserts have several rainstorms in one year, then dry weather for a few years. The differences occur because of the way air moves around the Earth. Sometimes a wind pushes clouds into a desert area and for a short time the water cycle is complete.

When it rains in a desert, a great quantity of water reaches the ground in a short time. Some

Water flows along a gully after rain in the North American desert.

passes straight into the dry sand, but the rest flows away fast and forms a river. Over the years these rivers form gullies called wadis. After rain, water may roar down the wadi, causing a **flash flood**. People who have camped in a wadi are in danger of being drowned if the rains arrive.

Deserts by the sea

It may seem strange to find deserts by the sea. Again, the explanation is a break in the water cycle. This can happen when the sea is cold. The ocean currents up the west coasts of South America and Africa come from the Antarctic Ocean and are very cold. Water does not evaporate from a cold sea, and so the air above does not take up any water vapour as it does when the water is warm.

Winds blow the cold, almost dry air onto the coast. In the daytime it warms up and draws any water from the land, and this helps to make the desert. At night, the land cools down. Some of the water in the air then condenses, forming droplets that make a fog. The Atacama and Namib Deserts have formed due to the water cycle being broken in this way.

Some other deserts by the sea, like those in Mexico and North Africa, are dry because winds blow the clouds away from the land.

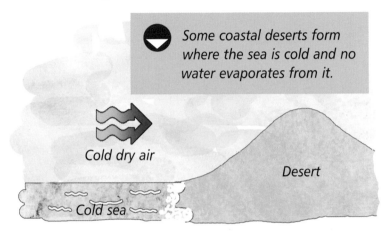

Some coastal deserts form where the sea is cold and no water evaporates from it.

Cold dry air

Cold sea

Desert

The Namib Desert begins right at the coast of Africa.

Why are some deserts so hot?

The answer to this is connected to the break in the water cycle. The dry air over a desert does not have any water droplets in it that can form clouds.

When clouds are present in any place, they form a barrier between the Sun and the surface of the Earth. When heat rays from the Sun strike a cloud, some are **absorbed** by the cloud and some are **reflected** back into space. The remaining heat rays pass through the cloud to the Earth's surface.

In the cloudless, dry air over a desert, nothing blocks the path of the Sun's heat rays. All of them strike the Earth's surface and make it very hot indeed. In Death Valley, in the Colorado Desert in North America, the ground may reach 80°C.

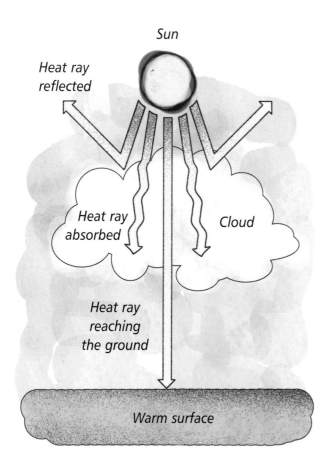

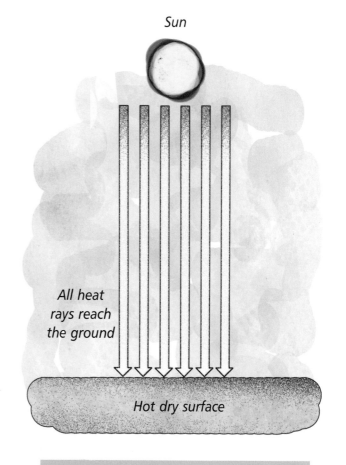

 When clouds are present, not all of the heat from the Sun's rays reaches the ground.

 With no clouds, all the heat from the Sun's rays reaches the ground.

In a hot desert, like Death Valley in the Colorado Desert, any plants look dry and dead. However, they have ways of surviving, which you will find out about on page 18.

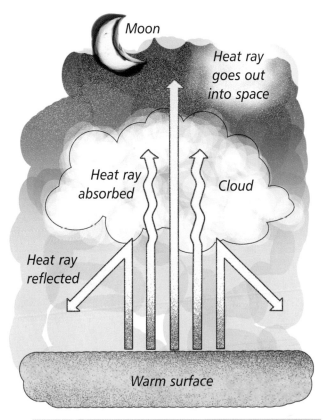

Moon

Heat ray goes out into space

Heat ray absorbed

Cloud

Heat ray reflected

Warm surface

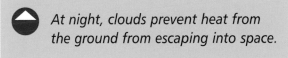

At night, clouds prevent heat from the ground from escaping into space.

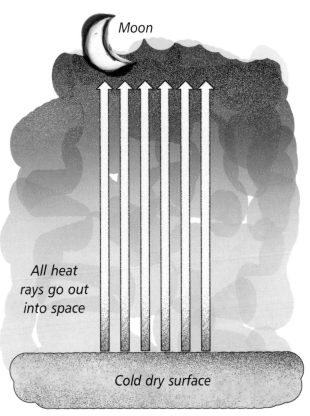

Moon

All heat rays go out into space

Cold dry surface

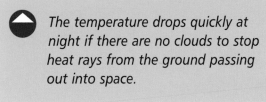

The temperature drops quickly at night if there are no clouds to stop heat rays from the ground passing out into space.

What happens to the heat at night?

When the ground receives heat, its temperature rises and it releases heat rays back into the air. These rays pass upwards in the air. If there are clouds above, they absorb some of the heat and reflect some of the rays back into the air below. These rays warm the air. You could say that the clouds act like a blanket, keeping the Earth warm.

In the desert, there are no clouds to absorb the heat rays coming from the ground and the rays pass out into space. As there is no blanket of cloud to keep the conditions warm, the temperature in the desert falls greatly at night. For example, in the Sahara, the daytime temperature may be 45°C, but at night it falls to −7°C.

Clothes for the desert

Clothes for the desert must protect your skin from the Sun's harmful rays. They must also stop you from becoming too hot and from losing too much moisture.

Many desert people wear a turban and flowing robes. The layers of clothing trap air between them, and the cloth and the air **insulate** the body from the desert heat. This means that they prevent the heat from reaching the body. At night, the insulating layers prevent the body's warmth from escaping into the cold desert air.

Because the clothes are loose-fitting, air can move over the skin. This feels cooling, as the movement of air causes some sweat to evaporate (change from liquid to water vapour).

However, the cloth keeps most of this water vapour in the air around the body. This prevents too much sweat from evaporating and leaving the body. Losing too much moisture could be very dangerous if there was little or no water to drink (see page 34).

Desert people, such as the Tuareg, wear a veil that can be pulled over their mouth and nose during a sandstorm. The veil acts as a filter. It lets air through to the nose and mouth, but keeps out sand grains, which could block the air passages in the body.

Can thick clothing keep out the heat?

You may think that thick clothing would make you hotter, not help to keep you cool. This activity shows how the scientific method is used to find an answer.

You need two plastic cups with lids, some thick woollen cloth, scissors, sticky tape, a clock, two ice cubes that are the same size.

1 Cut out a strip of cloth and wrap it around one of the cups. Fix the cloth in place with sticky tape.

2 Cut out a strip of cloth and stick it on top of one of the lids.

3 Put an ice cube in each cup and close the lids.

4 Put the cups in a warm place, such as a sunny windowsill.

5 After ten minutes, look in the cups and examine the ice cubes.

6 Close the lids and leave for another ten minutes. Then have another look.

7 Repeat step 6 until an hour has passed. Then pour out the contents of each cup.

Which cube melted more than the other?

Wrap and secure with tape.

Remember to check regularly and note changes.

Many people who make expeditions into the desert do not wear robes, but choose clothes like these to give them the protection they need.

Wide-brimmed hat keeps sun off face and neck.

Bandana can be wrapped around head in a sandstorm to protect the nose and mouth.

Sunglasses or goggles protect eyes.

Like many people who live in the desert, Bedouin wear loose-fitting robes to insulate their bodies from the heat.

Loose-fitting shirt and baggy trousers allow air to circulate.

Hard-wearing leather boots protect feet on expeditions over rocks and gravel. Felt inside provides extra insulation from hot desert rocks.

Eye protection

The bright sunlight is reflected off the dust in the air and the rocks on the ground. This creates glare, which dazzles the eyes and makes it difficult to see clearly. If you cannot see where you are going in the desert light, you may soon be lost. A simple way to reduce glare is to rub charcoal from a campfire into the skin below the eyes. The charcoal absorbs light that strikes the skin around the eyes and prevents it entering the eyes.

People setting out on an expedition into the desert should take sunglasses with them. Some desert travellers prefer goggles, as these also keep sand out of the eyes in a sandstorm.

Going without clothes

The San people of the Kalahari and Namib and the Aborigines of the Australian deserts wear very few clothes. They can survive in this way because their dark-coloured skin gives them extra protection from the Sun's harmful **ultraviolet** rays. The skin contains large amounts of a **pigment** called melanin. This absorbs the ultraviolet rays, and prevents them going deeper into the skin and causing damage such as blistering and burning. The large amounts of melanin make the skin black.

You may think that, since the San and Aborigines have skin exposed to the air, they lose a great deal of water through sweat. In fact, they manage to control the amount of sweat they lose by moving steadily, without rushing. When someone moves quickly, their muscles produce a great deal of heat. The body responds by sweating (and losing lots of water) to lose the heat. Moving without rushing keeps sweating to a minimum. Even people who are clothed can reduce the amount of sweat they produce by moving as the San and Aborigines do.

 These San hunters in the Kalahari are resting in the desert heat while they study animal tracks in the sand.

Investigating desert plants

In most parts of a desert you will see some plants, even if it has not rained for months. You may see thorn bushes and tufts of dried-up grasses. In the American deserts you will see cacti. In places where water flows after rain, there may be a few trees. Many of the plants may look dead, but in fact they are **dormant**. Inside their bodies, **life processes** are taking place very slowly, so little water is used up until it rains again.

Most plants collect water with their roots. Some desert plants, such as cacti, have roots that grow outwards, just below the surface of the sand, to collect as much water as they can when rain falls. Other plants, such as trees, have roots that grow far down to collect water that has sunk deep into the sand.

Desert plants have ways of holding on to the water they have collected. They may store it in their roots or in their stems.

After rain, huge numbers of plants push through the wet soil and burst into flower.

Surviving as seeds

The plants that suddenly appear after desert rain have grown from seeds. They grow quickly and make more seeds before they dry up and die. The seeds live on in the soil, because they have a little water inside them and have thick skins to stop them losing it. When the next rains arrive, the seeds take in water, swell up and **germinate**. Again, the new plants grow quickly and make more seeds before they dry up and die.

These flowers appeared after rain in a desert region of southern Africa.

How much water do seeds need to germinate?

You are going to do a **fair test**. For your results to be accurate, you must measure the amounts of water carefully and keep a record of them.

You need three dishes of sand about 2cm deep, 30 mustard seeds, a beaker of water, a measuring cylinder.

1 Place 10 seeds in the sand in each dish.

2 Give the first dish about 20cm³ of water.

3 Give the second dish about 50cm³ of water.

4 Give the third dish about 100cm³ of water.

5 Leave each dish for a few days and look for signs of germination. If a seed germinates, it will send out a root and then send out a shoot.

6 Once you have found that seeds will germinate when given a certain amount of water, you could try the test again – but this time give each dish a smaller amount of water than the one before.

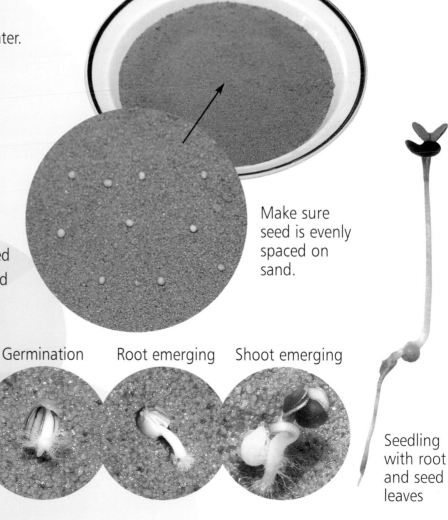

Make sure seed is evenly spaced on sand.

Germination   Root emerging   Shoot emerging

Seedling with root and seed leaves

How plants solve desert problems

Plants need water to make food and to take in **minerals** from the soil. They take in water through their roots and it moves up into all parts of the plant due to a process called **transpiration**. In this process water evaporates from the leaves and more water is drawn through the plant.

In a hot, dry desert, water could evaporate from the leaves of a plant so fast that it would soon use up all its water. Plants that live in hot, dry deserts have solved the problem in different ways. For example, some have leaves with tough, leathery skins, through which only small amounts of water can pass.

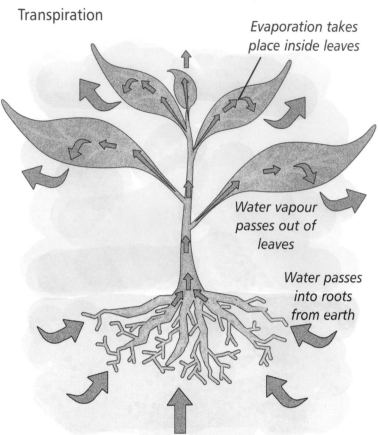

Transpiration

Evaporation takes place inside leaves

Water vapour passes out of leaves

Water passes into roots from earth

The saguaro, which grows only in parts of the North American deserts, is the largest type of cactus. It can reach 21 metres high.

Cacti do not have any leaves. They lose their water through small holes in their stems. The spines around a cactus also trap a layer of air close to the holes and this slows down evaporation. If the cacti did not have their spines, air would sweep over their waxy surfaces, speed up evaporation and dry them out.

The pebble plant, of the Kalahari Desert, has two thick waxy leaves which it keeps close to the ground. This prevents winds drying out the leaves.

There is another way in which plants can lose water. They can lose it to animals that bite into them to get a drink. Cacti defend themselves with spines. Some plants produce chemicals which make the water taste bad or even make it poisonous. Animals and humans learn to avoid these plants.

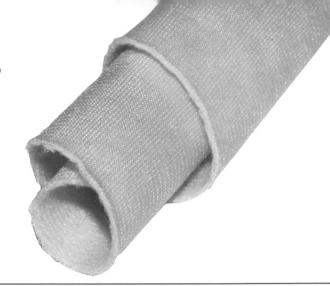

Does curling up hold on to water?

Some plants such as grasses curl up their leaves in dry weather. This is said to help them hold on to water. When scientists want to investigate an idea, they sometimes use models. In this activity you use model leaves made from pieces of cloth.

You need cloth, scissors, a beaker of water, a tray, a warm place such as a sunny windowsill

1 Cut out two pieces of cloth. You may make them leaf-shaped, but they must be the same size.

2 Dip one 'leaf' in the beaker of water and hold it over the beaker until it has stopped dripping.

3 Spread the leaf out on the tray.

4 Repeat step 2 with the second leaf.

5 Place the second leaf on the tray, but roll it up.

6 Put the tray in a warm place such as a sunny window for an hour. Then check the dampness of each leaf. You will have to uncurl the second leaf to check its dampness.

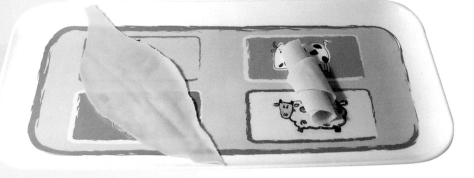

Walking in the desert

People should walk at a steady pace and not rush. They should stop about every hour and rest in some shade for up to ten minutes. This stops them getting too hot and helps keep sweating to a minimum. They need to conserve as much water in their bodies as they can.

A rock or a hill may cast some shade, or people could make a small tent with some cloth and a stick. If resting near rocks, they should look out for snakes, which may be resting there too.

Some people rest through the day and walk at night. It is much cooler then and they can keep themselves warm simply by walking. The sky is clear at night in the desert, so there is light from the Moon and stars. At full Moon you may see well for about 100 metres. However, people travelling at night must watch for desert animals, like snakes and scorpions, as many are **nocturnal**.

Sun low in sky at early morning or late afternoon

Heat ray spreads out over a large area of ground

Sun at midday

Heat ray only covers a small area of ground

 It is hottest at midday because the Sun's rays beat down on a smaller area than at other times. The ground heats up and passes some of its heat back into the air above it. It is dangerous to stay out in the midday Sun.

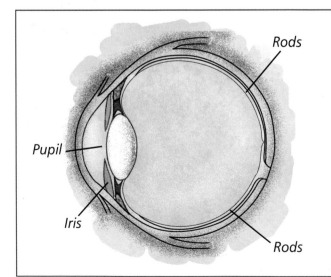

Rods

Pupil

Iris

Rods

How our eyes see in the dark

In bed at night, when you first switch off the light, everything seems black. But after a few minutes you may be able to see dark shapes and objects. Two things happen to help us see in the dark. A chemical change takes place in light receptors at the back of the eyes, called **rods**. And muscles in the **iris** pull together to make the **pupil** wider so that more light can reach the rods.

These tourists visiting the Namib Desert are walking along a ridge, to get the best view of the landscape.

Dangerous wadi

If you walk across sand, your boots sink into it and you soon become tired. It's easier if you can find rocky or pebbly ground to walk on, such as the floor of a wadi. A wadi with steep sides also gives some shade. However, a wadi can be a dangerous place to walk.

The danger comes from flash floods. A rainstorm many kilometres away may cause water to rush down the wadi. The water may be over a metre deep and travel very fast. It lifts pebbles and rocks from the wadi floor and carries them in the current. People walking in the wadi may be caught in the rushing water. They may be knocked over by the current and beaten to death by the moving rocks. So, before walking in a wadi, you need to be sure that, if a flood happened, you could climb very quickly up the wadi sides.

Safer high ground

In many places, ridges of land rise above the desert floor. These are not sand dunes but hard rock, and it is easy to walk along the top of them. From this high ground large areas of the desert can be seen and you can look for landmarks.

Between the sand dunes

The wind blows the sand into heaps called dunes. Some can reach a height of 300 metres. The way the wind blows on the sand affects the way the dunes form. Some dunes are over 100 kilometres long and are arranged in lines. There are long straight valleys between the dunes through which people can travel.

Travelling by camel

Camels are used to transport people, their homes, and goods, such as salt. A camel can carry a load of about 100 kilograms – the weight of about three ten-year-old children.

A one-humped camel is called a dromedary, and a two-humped camel is called a bactrian camel. The dromedary is used in the African and Australian deserts, and the bactrian camel in the Gobi Desert.

Camels tend to be bad-tempered. They often spit at people who come too close. They can also give a powerful kick. If a camel knocks someone over, it may sit on them and crush them with a hard pad on its chest called the brisket. Camels also bite.

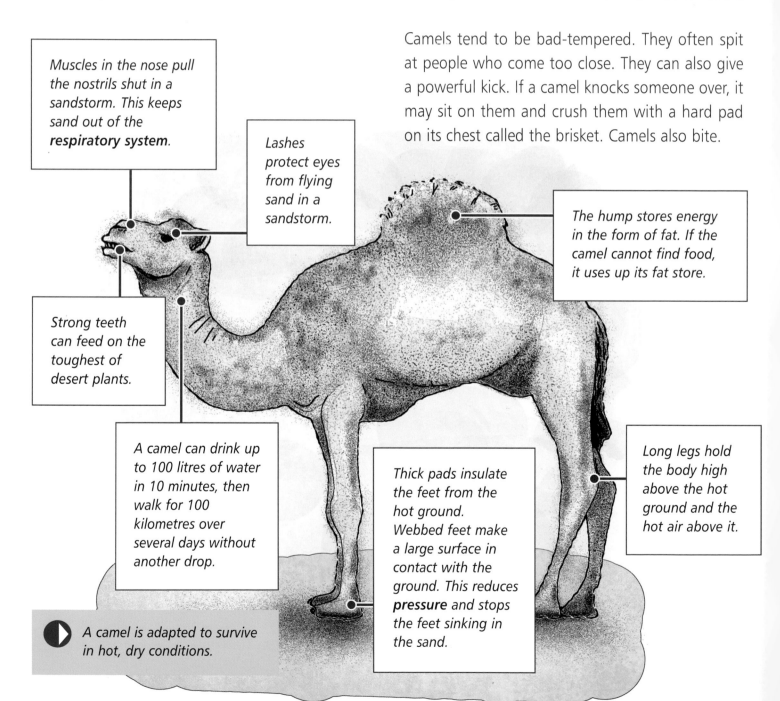

Muscles in the nose pull the nostrils shut in a sandstorm. This keeps sand out of the **respiratory system***.*

Lashes protect eyes from flying sand in a sandstorm.

The hump stores energy in the form of fat. If the camel cannot find food, it uses up its fat store.

Strong teeth can feed on the toughest of desert plants.

A camel can drink up to 100 litres of water in 10 minutes, then walk for 100 kilometres over several days without another drop.

Thick pads insulate the feet from the hot ground. Webbed feet make a large surface in contact with the ground. This reduces **pressure** *and stops the feet sinking in the sand.*

Long legs hold the body high above the hot ground and the hot air above it.

▶ *A camel is adapted to survive in hot, dry conditions.*

Investigating feet in the sand

This activity investigates the part of the camel's foot that is in contact with the sand. To make the investigation simple, model feet (blocks of wood) are used.

You need a bowl of sand, two blocks of wood the same height (e.g. 8cm) – one with a larger surface area than the other, a flat piece of wood three-quarters the width of the bowl, a weight of about 1kg, a tape measure.

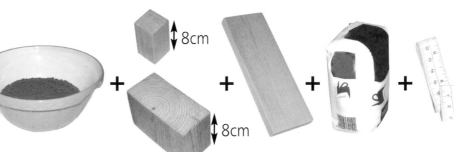

1 Make sure that the space between the sand and the top of the bowl is the same as the height of your two wooden blocks.

2 Place the large block on the sand, and rest the flat piece of wood on top of the block and the edge of the bowl.

3 Put the weight on it and see how far the 'foot' sinks into the sand. Remove the 'foot' and measure the depth of the 'footprint'.

4 Repeat steps 1-3 with the smaller block.

You should find that the 'foot' with the small surface area sinks further into the sand than the one with the larger surface area. Does this help you explain why a camel has webbed feet?

Measure the depth of each 'footprint'.

25

Travelling by truck

In the past, camels were used to carry the equipment needed on expeditions. Today, trucks are often used. Usually, two or more vehicles travel together so that, if one gets stuck in the sand, another can pull it out.

 A truck can travel off the road, on rough ground like the stony, sandy floor of the desert. However, care must be taken not to get stuck in the sand. If this happens, the wheels just spin, instead of pushing on the sand to move the vehicle forwards.

Loading up

When people load up a truck, they need to think about its centre of **gravity**. This will make sure that the vehicle does not topple over when driving along a slope.

Every object has a centre of gravity, a point from which the object's weight pulls down. If you tip the object slightly, as shown in diagram b, its weight still pulls down through its base. When you let go, the object will fall back to its original position.

If you tip the object so much that its weight pulls down through its side (diagram c), and then let go, the object will fall on its side.

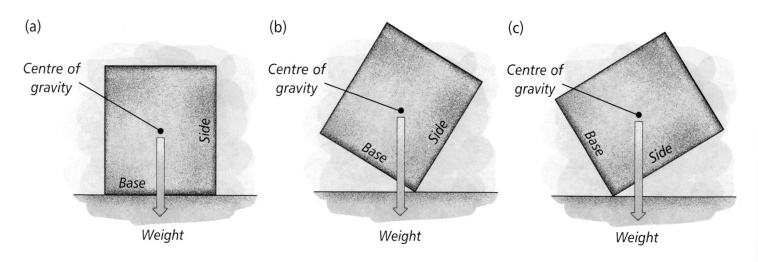

(a)

Centre of gravity

Side

Base

Weight

(b)

Centre of gravity

Base

Side

Weight

(c)

Centre of gravity

Base

Side

Weight

Loading a model truck

An object's centre of gravity is where most of its weight is found. When a truck is not loaded, most of its weight is low down by the wheels. When it is loaded, its centre of gravity is higher. In this activity you test what difference a higher centre of gravity makes.

You need a box to represent a truck, a tray, modelling clay, wooden bricks, a plastic bag, a tape measure, sticky tape.

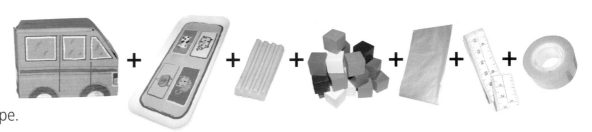

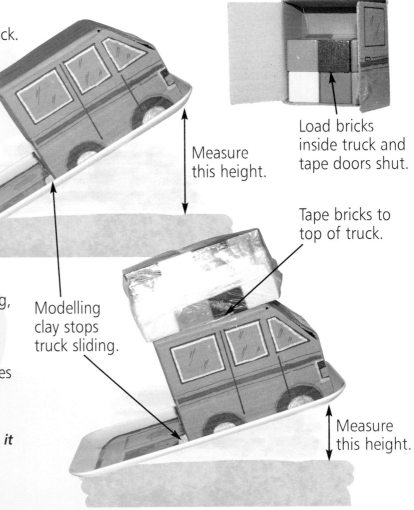

1 If you wish, decorate the box to look like a truck.

2 Put the truck on the end of the tray and position pieces of modelling clay to stop it sliding when you tip the tray.

3 Put some bricks inside the truck. Then raise one end of the tray until the truck topples over. Measure the height of the slope.

4 Take out the bricks, put them in a plastic bag, and stick them on the roof of the truck.

5 Raise one end of the tray until the truck topples over. Measure the height of the slope again.

How do you think a truck should be loaded to stop it toppling over easily on a slope?

Measure this height.

Load bricks inside truck and tape doors shut.

Tape bricks to top of truck.

Modelling clay stops truck sliding.

Measure this height.

Finding the way

The wind is responsible for the shape of the dunes and for the way rocks have been eroded. Particular shaped rocks can be used as landmarks.

When the air is clear in a desert, you can see far around you. This helps you look for landmarks such as cliffs or star-shaped sand dunes. Dunes like this form where there are huge amounts of sand and the wind blows from several directions. Star-shaped dunes tend to stay in one place for up to 200 years.

In some deserts the wind tends to blow from one direction, such as north or west. This wind is called the **prevailing wind**. Sometimes a prevailing wind pushes sand into crescent-shaped humps called barchan dunes. The horns of these dunes point away from the direction from which the wind is blowing. So, for example, if you know that the prevailing wind blows from the west, the horns of the dunes will be pointing east. And you can work out north and south.

If there are no barchan dunes in your desert, and you do not have a compass, you can still find north and south in the day and at night, by looking at the Sun or Moon.

Star-shaped dune

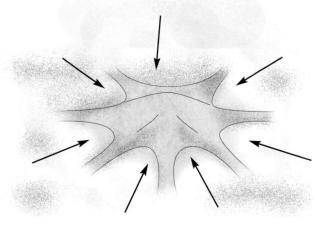

Wind direction

Barchan dune

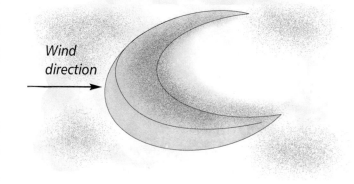

Wind direction

Can you find directions using the Sun?

The **Solar System** formed from a swirling cloud of gas and dust. A huge ball of gas at the centre became the Sun. As planets and moons formed from dust and gases, they took on a spinning motion. The Earth spins once every day and this is why it seems to us that the Sun moves across the sky, rising in the east and setting in the west. We can use the changing positions of the Sun to find directions.

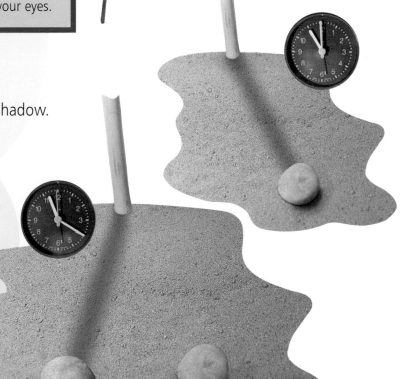

You need a sunny day, some level ground, a stick about a metre long, two pebbles, a clock.

 +  +

Warning!

Never look directly at the Sun! It can damage your eyes.

1 Push the stick into the ground so that it stands up vertically.

2 Find the shadow cast by the stick.

3 Put a pebble on the ground at the tip of the shadow.

4 After 20 minutes repeat steps 2 and 3 with the second pebble.

5 Stand with your back to the Sun and put the tip of each foot close to a pebble. If you are in the Northern Hemisphere you will now be facing north (or south if you are in the Southern Hemisphere). You may like to check your accuracy by using a compass.

Can you find directions using the Moon?

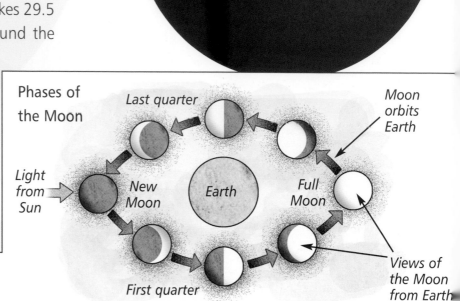

As well as spinning, planets constantly orbit (travel round) the Sun, and moons orbit some of the planets. The Earth has one Moon, which takes 29.5 days for its orbit. As the Moon moves round the Earth, it is lit by different amounts of sunlight. Stages in the path of the Moon around the Earth are called the **phases of the Moon**.

Some scientists say that the phases of the Moon can be used to find directions. Try checking out the claim in this activity.

You need a clear night when the Moon is at a quarter moon phase.

Phases of the Moon

Moon orbits Earth

Light from Sun

New Moon

Earth

Full Moon

First quarter

Last quarter

Views of the Moon from Earth

1 Look at the quarter moon and find its horns.

2 In your mind, make a line between the two horns.

3 In your mind, continue the line down to the horizon.

4 If you are in the Northern Hemisphere, the point where the line touches the horizon is roughly south. If you are in the Southern Hemisphere, the point shows the rough direction of north.

5 Check the accuracy of this method with a compass.

Making a shelter

You may need a shelter at night, to protect you from the cold, or a shelter for the daytime, to rest away from the desert Sun. You may sometimes need a shelter to protect you from a fierce sandstorm.

Building materials

Building materials in a desert are sand, rocks, dead trees and the living shoots of bushes. These can be used with cloths carried on the expedition to make one of these simple shelters.

- Gather some rocks and make them into a circular wall. Place shoots of bushes or tree branches across the top, and spread cloth over them.

- Roll two dead tree trunks until they lie almost next to each other. Dig out the sand between them to make a hollow. Then make a roof from branches and cloth.

- Use branches, shoots and cloth to make a lean-to shelter against a large boulder. The roof of the shelter must be facing the direction of the prevailing wind so that the wind pushes it against the rock. (If it is built facing the opposite direction, the wind may get under the roof and carry it away.)

In a sandstorm, flying sand can hurt your skin and eyes and get into your airways. It is best to shelter until the storm is over.

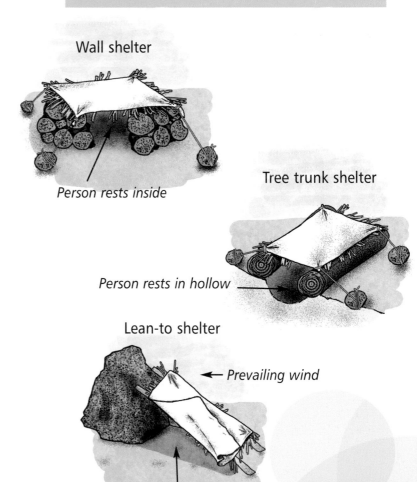

Wall shelter

Person rests inside

Tree trunk shelter

Person rests in hollow

Lean-to shelter

← *Prevailing wind*

Person rests under here

Keeping cool or warm

During the day the sides of the shelter need to be open a little, to let air circulate inside. This helps keep the shelter cool. At night the sides need to be closed, to keep in the heat.

If you are camping at night, you will also need to make a fire to keep warm and cook food. As there are often few woody plants in a desert, it does not make sense only to look for wood when a camp is made. It is better to collect wood throughout the day, wherever you notice it as you are travelling.

Heating inside a shelter

There are plenty of stones in a desert and some can be put round the fire to heat up. Once hot, they can be rolled or carried on pieces of wood into a shelter and used to warm the air inside. If there is a space under the beds in the shelter, the stones can be put there. The heat rising from them keeps people warm as they sleep.

 These Bedouin people in the Sinai Desert have gathered around their campfire to drink tea.

This ger in Outer Mongolia looks plain and simple from the outside ...

Shelters made by desert people

The San of the Kalahari build simple shelters from thin, bendy branches. The branches are tied together to form a dome. The sides of the dome are covered in leaves to make the shelter shady in the day, warm at night, and windproof all the time.

The Bedouin make large tents. The cloth is made from the wool of camels, sheep and goats. Flaps in the sides of the tent can be opened or closed to control the temperature inside. More sheets of cloth are used to divide the tents into several rooms.

The Mongols make large round tents called gers. A wooden framework is covered with thick cloth made from wool. The main function of this shelter is to keep people warm in the cold desert. At the centre of the ger a fire is kept burning, for cooking and to keep the inside warm. There is a chimney in the top of the ger to let out the smoke.

... But inside, the ger is colourful and homely.

Where to find water

All your body's life processes need water. If your body does not receive enough water to keep these processes going, they stop and you die. Water enters your body in drinks and food, but you also lose water in your breath, in sweat, in urine and with the solid wastes from your digestive system. You must keep taking in water to replace what you lose.

At home, you may lose a litre of water if you rest all day, and up to three litres if you move about. In a desert, a person sweats more and may lose up to five litres of water in a day. If a person walked across a desert during the day without having a drink, they would be dead by sunset. People on an expedition must work out how much water they will need each day and carry it with them on their camels or trucks.

The oasis

Far out in a desert you may find trees growing round a pool of water. This place is called an oasis. It can provide water for drinking.

This oasis in the Sahara Desert has been developed so that food can be grown there.

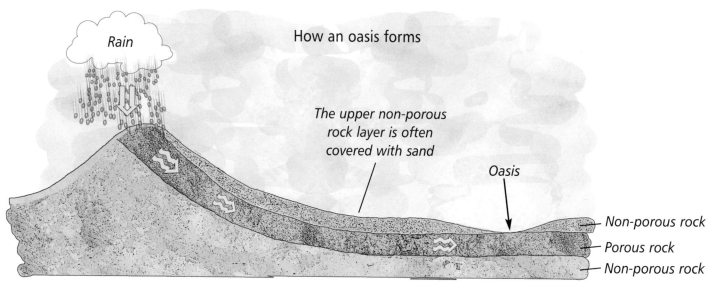

How an oasis forms

Rain

The upper non-porous rock layer is often covered with sand

Oasis

Non-porous rock

Porous rock

Non-porous rock

An oasis forms because of the way two types of rock are found under the desert. They are **porous** rock, which lets water soak into it, and non-porous rock, which does not let water through. They are arranged in layers, as the diagram shows. These kinds of rock may cover hundreds of kilometres under the desert and reach distant mountains.

If it rains frequently in the mountains, the water soaks into the porous rock but stops when it reaches the non-porous rock. It then flows through the porous rock under the desert. In a place in the desert where the porous rock reaches the surface, a pool of water forms and plants can grow in the damp soil round it.

A mirage

A mirage is a trick of the light. It makes you think there is a pool of water in the desert when there is really no water. A mirage is made in the following way.

There is a layer of hot air close to the ground and a layer of cooler air above it. Light shining from the sky moves through the cool air in a straight line. But when it reaches the warmer air, it changes direction and shines upwards again, as if it had been reflected. Anyone looking at this light sees it appear to come from a pool of water.

People desperate for water have followed mirages and perished.

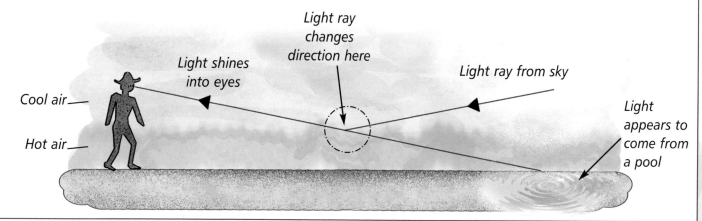

Light ray changes direction here

Light shines into eyes

Light ray from sky

Cool air

Hot air

Light appears to come from a pool

Obtaining water from air

Air contains water in the form of water vapour, and warm air can hold more water vapour than cold air. At night, the warm desert air cools down and must lose some of its water vapour. It does this in a process called condensation. Some of the water vapour turns into liquid water and settles on the ground. If a large cloth is spread out on desert grass in the evening, water vapour will condense on it overnight. In the morning, the cloth can then be squeezed over a cup to collect the water.

Some beetles let dew form on them at night, so that they can get a drink by morning.

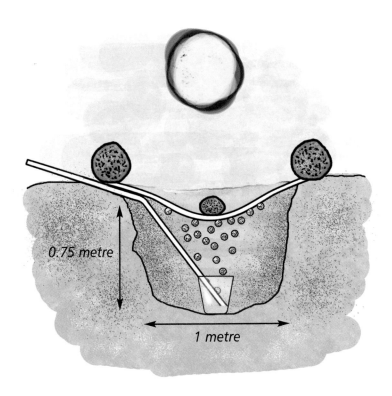

0.75 metre

1 metre

A solar still

A solar still can be set up at a desert camp to provide about 1.5 litres of water in 24 hours. A container with a plastic drinking tube is placed in the bottom, and a clear plastic sheet is fixed over the top of the hole. A stone placed in the centre of the sheet makes it dip down over the container.

The Sun's rays pass through the plastic and warm the air inside. This warms the sand in the hole and makes any water that is present evaporate, forming water vapour. At night the vapour condenses on the underside of the plastic, flows towards the centre and drips into the container. The water is removed by sucking on the tube.

Some desert plants can be put in the bottom of the still so that water can evaporate from them too.

Make a model solar still

'Solar' means 'to do with the Sun' and a 'still' is a device for **distilling** a liquid. (This means making the liquid evaporate and then condense again.) You can see how the still works by making a model one.

You need a large bowl, a cup, some clingfilm, a pebble, some very warm water (from the hot tap).

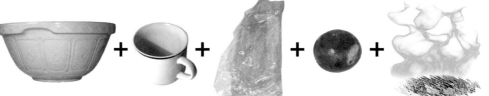

1 Put the cup in the middle of the bowl.

2 Pour the warm water around the cup.

3 Cover the top of the bowl with clingfilm and put the pebble in the middle so the clingfilm dips down over the cup.

4 Look at the still every few minutes. You should see water condense on the underside of the clingfilm and drip into the cup.

5 How do you think the temperature of the water will affect how much you can collect? Work out an investigation to test your idea.

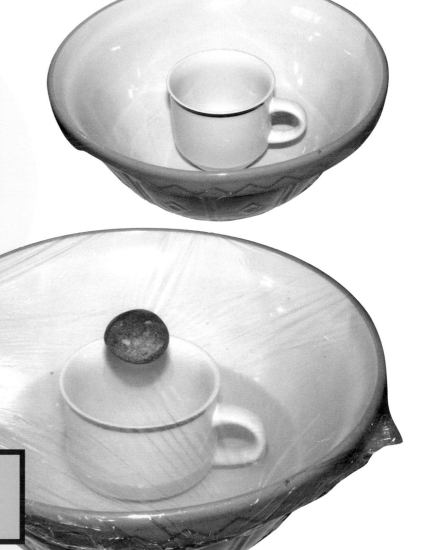

Warning!
You will need adult supervision when using very hot water.

Staying healthy and safe

The main danger to health in the desert is **dehydration**. This is loss of water from the body. Desert travellers should try to conserve as much water in their bodies as possible, in case something happens to stop them reaching their destination on time. For example, a sandstorm can keep people in a camp away from water for a few days.

The main way to conserve water is to reduce sweating. We have seen how this can be done by choosing loose-fitting clothes, moving steadily without rushing, resting regularly, staying in the shade and travelling at night. Another thing to remember is that you lose water from the lining of your mouth if you breathe with your mouth open – so in the desert you should only breathe through your nose. Also, digestion uses up water, and so you should eat less in the desert. Plants should be eaten in preference to meat, as many plant foods contain more water.

These wild cucumbers in the Kalahari Desert are an example of **gourds**. They are a source of food and water.

Food and water from plants

Some desert plants provide food. For example, fruits from the date palm can be eaten raw. Acacia leaves and shoots can be boiled, to make them edible. Acacia seeds can be roasted, or ground up into a flour to make a porridge.

Gourds grow in many deserts. Their shoots can be chewed to provide a drink of water. Gourd leaves and fruits can be boiled and eaten, and their seeds can be roasted.

Beware! The water that many cacti store in their stems has poisons in it, to prevent animals (and humans) drinking it.

Making sure that water is safe

You need to take care that the water you drink is safe. You may find a water hole – a hollow in a river bed that has not dried up. Beware:

- If lots of animal bones are found near a water hole, it may mean that the water is poisonous.

- The water may contain **microbes**, which cause diseases such as dysentery. These diseases make the digestive system discharge large amounts of water as diarrhoea. This further dehydrates the body and increases the chance of death. Water must be boiled for at least ten minutes to kill the microbes.

- Large carnivores like lions may drink at water holes. They could attack.

A date palm tree can produce up to 250kg of dates each year, for 100 years or more.

Getting enough salt

The body contains many chemicals, which help it survive. A vital one is salt. Without salt, the nervous system fails to work properly and you feel dizzy and sick. The muscles are also affected and you develop muscle cramps. People on desert expeditions take salt tablets in water, to replace the salt they lose through sweating.

Look out for scorpions

Scorpions have eight legs and a pair of pincers, with which they hold their prey. On the tip of their tail is a sting. It contains poison, which is injected into the prey to kill it. The poison is also used in self-defence. The poison of some scorpions is so strong that it can kill a human.

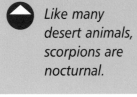 Like many desert animals, scorpions are nocturnal.

Scorpions hide under rocks in the day and come out at night to find food. People travelling at night should look out for them. Also, in camps, all boots and shoes should be shaken in the morning, to check that a scorpion has not climbed inside.

Stay away from snakes

A cobra has loose folds of skin around its neck, which can be spread out to make a 'hood' when the snake is alarmed.

Many desert snakes have colours that give them **camouflage** and make them difficult to see. Some snakes have venom strong enough to kill people. Most snakes are active at night. During the day they can be found coiled up by logs.

If you discover a snake you must stand still and let it move away. If the snake stays still, you must go round it – at a distance. Snakes tend to attack if you go near, so the rule is to keep away.

How desert animals survive

During the hottest part of the day almost all desert animals hide away in the shade. Many rest in burrows underground. Even a few centimetres below the surface of the sand the temperature is much lower.

Some animals live and move about below the surface, by swimming through the sand. These include reptiles called legless skinks, which look like small eels, and mammals like the golden mole, which hunt them.

Close-up of capillaries

⬆ A golden mole kills its prey. Usually, a golden mole moves along just below the surface of the sand, and so you only see the marks it makes.

⬆ The heart pumps warm blood from inside the jackrabbit's body through capillaries in its ears. Heat passes from the blood into the air and the cool blood returns to the jackrabbit's body.

Big ears

The fenec of Africa, the jackrabbit of North America and the rabbit-eared bandicoot of Australia are desert animals with large ears. These help to keep the animals cool. In all animals, the blood carries heat around the body. In the ears of these desert animals there is a large network of small blood vessels called **capillaries**, all near to the surface of the skin. As the blood flows through them, it loses its heat into the air.

Kangaroos have capillaries close to the skin surface of their forearms, and can use these to lose heat.

Increasing evaporation

When your sweat evaporates, it takes heat from your skin and the blood flowing beneath it. This helps to keep you cool. Other mammals sweat to keep cool, but many also pant. Panting causes evaporation to take place in the mouth and cools the blood that flows close by. But panting also makes heat, as the chest muscles work to draw air in and out of the body.

Desert birds draw air in and out without making so much heat. They just use the muscles in their throat to make the throat flutter, and this makes the air move. The moving air causes water to evaporate from the mouth.

A desert kangaroo licks saliva onto its forearms, which have a network of capillaries. As the water in the saliva evaporates, the blood passing through the forearms is cooled down.

The tortoise covers its head and neck in saliva. If it is really hot, it also releases urine onto its back legs, to increase evaporation from its body.

Conserving water

Animals also need to conserve water in their bodies. One way to lessen the amount of water they lose is to stay in a burrow. In the cool of a burrow they do not need to pant.

Staying in a burrow helps to conserve water in another way too. When water vapour leaves the body in a burrow, it stays in the air and makes it humid. The humid air slows down evaporation from the animal's body.

Testing the effect of a burrow

You can use models to test how resting in a burrow helps an animal to conserve water.

You need a cardboard box with a lid, two identical pieces of sponge, two pieces of plastic, water, a measuring cylinder.

1 Make a small hole in the box. The box is the burrow.

2 Put it on a sunny windowsill.

3 The sponge pieces are two animals of the same kind. Soak them in water. Then let the excess water drip off them.

4 Put one piece of plastic in the box, place one of the 'animals' on it, and close the lid.

5 Place the second piece of plastic and the other 'animal' on top of the box.

6 Leave the 'burrow' and the 'animals' for a few hours.

7 Squeeze each sponge over the measuring cylinder and record the two amounts of water you collect. Which 'animal' conserved more water?

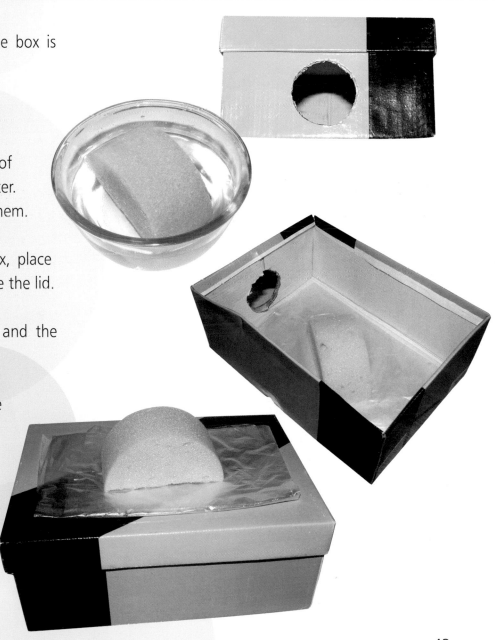

Rescue

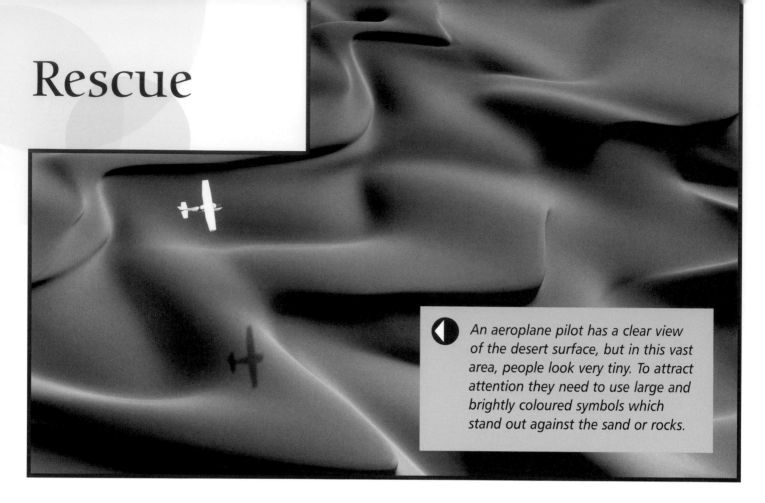

An aeroplane pilot has a clear view of the desert surface, but in this vast area, people look very tiny. To attract attention they need to use large and brightly coloured symbols which stand out against the sand or rocks.

An aeroplane is sent to search for people who do not return when expected from a desert expedition. Aeroplanes cover large areas quickly and the surface of the desert can be seen easily from above, provided there are no sandstorms. People who need to be rescued must make themselves as visible as possible.

If your truck breaks down you should stay with the vehicle, as it is easy to see from an aircraft. In the evening the vehicle's lights can be switched on to attract attention.

People without a vehicle could arrange stones into lines, circles, triangles, squares or letters. An orderly arrangement stands out from the normal scattered arrangement of rocks on the desert floor. The symbols you make must be not less than two metres long.

People on expeditions may carry rolled-up rescue panels – pieces of brightly coloured material. When they are unrolled, they are two metres long and a half metre wide. They can be joined together to make symbols which can be seen from the air.

Emergency ground to air signals

F = need food and water

M = need medical supplies

I = serious injury

↗ = I am moving this way

X = cannot move

A = yes or affirmative

N = no

JL = I don't understand

Which colours make the clearest signals?

When some colours are put together, one seems to stand out, or contrast sharply with the other. This makes it more visible to the eye. You can find out which colours are most visible to your eye in desert conditions by trying this fair test.

You need yellow or buff paper, a selection of brightly coloured lightweight cloth material.

1 Predict which material you think will stand out most against the desert colour. Put the materials in order, starting with the one you think will be easiest to see.

2 Choose an emergency signal and cut it out from each material. Make sure that all the symbols are the same size.

3 Mount each symbol on yellow or buff paper.

4 Set up two mounted symbols at the end of a large room and see which stands out more.

5 Repeat step 4 with all the symbols.

6 Compare the symbols that you picked as standing out more, to find the best one. Were your predictions right?

The end of the journey

At the end of a journey, people often feel that they have learnt a lot along the way. How did you get on, visiting the deserts in this book and trying out your science skills? Can you explain how the water cycle is broken to make a desert? Do you know why camels can cross sand easily, or how to load a truck to prevent it tipping up on a slope?

About a third of the Earth's land surface is covered by desert. Perhaps one day you will make a real journey to visit such a place. In the meantime, part of the desert may visit you. Winds blow dust from the deserts far across the Earth. The dust on your windowsill could have started its journey in the desert.

Glossary

absorb — take in. (The water in a cloud absorbs heat energy and becomes warmer.)

camouflage — a way of blending in with the surroundings in order not to be easily seen. This may include having colours the same as the surroundings.

capillaries — small tubes with very thin walls through which blood flows in all parts of an animal's body.

condense — change from a gas to a liquid.

dehydration — a condition of the body in which it has too little water to work properly and stay healthy.

desert storms — periods of high wind, heavy rainfall and thunder and lightning in the desert.

distil — separate a liquid from the substances dissolved in it by making the liquid change into a gas and then condense again.

dormant — inactive. During the dormant stage of its life, a plant does not take in water, make food or grow.

evaporate — change from a liquid into a gas.

expedition — a journey made for a particular purpose, such as to find out about the plants and animals in a place.

fair test — an investigation in which only one thing is varied. In a fair test of the effect of water on two sets of seeds, different amounts of water are used, but all other things such as warmth and the amount of light must be the same for both sets.

flash flood — a flood which suddenly develops over a small area, such as a dry river bed, due to heavy rain.

germinate — send out a root to collect water and a shoot to make food. This is the action of the tiny plant inside a seed as the seed coat breaks open.

gourd — a fruit with a hard skin and a soft inside, containing a large amount of water.

gravity — the force that pulls objects down towards the centre of the Earth. Gravity is also a force which exists between any two objects in the universe, but is often too weak to make the objects move together.

insulate — stop the movement of heat. It can also mean to stop the movement of electricity.

iris — the coloured muscular ring at the front of the eye, which surrounds the round black spot called the pupil.

life processes	processes or changes that take place in a living thing, to keep it alive.
microbes	tiny forms of life that can only be seen with a powerful microscope.
minerals	substances in the soil that a plant needs for good health. The minerals dissolve in water in the soil and are taken into the plant by the roots.
nocturnal	sleeping through the day and active at night.
oasis	a place in the desert where water is found. Some plants may grow there.
observation	looking carefully at the way something is, or the way in which something happens.
phases of the Moon	the different shapes of the sunlit parts of the Moon as the Moon travels in its orbit around the Earth.
pigment	a substance that gives colour to the body of a human, animal or plant.
porous	with small spaces inside, which can take up water.
pressure	the push of a force on an area of a surface.
prevailing wind	the wind that blows most often in a particular region.
pupil	the round black spot at the front of the eye. It is a hole at the centre of the iris through which light passes into the back of the eye.
reflected	turned back from a surface.
respiratory system	the part of the body that takes in oxygen from the air and gives out carbon dioxide. This includes the nose, windpipe and lungs.
rods	tiny parts of the eye which are sensitive to small amounts of light.
sand dunes	hills of sand that have been built up by the wind blowing across the desert.
Solar System	the Sun and all the things around it in space (e.g. planets, asteroids, comets) which are pulled by its gravity.
transpiration	a process in which water is lost by evaporation from surfaces of a plant shoot, such as those of the leaves.
ultraviolet	a form of energy. It travels as waves across space and through the air. It has a shorter wavelength than light and cannot be detected by our eyes.
wadi	a deep, narrow valley in the desert. It carries fast-flowing water after rain.
water vapour	the gas which water forms when it evaporates.

Index